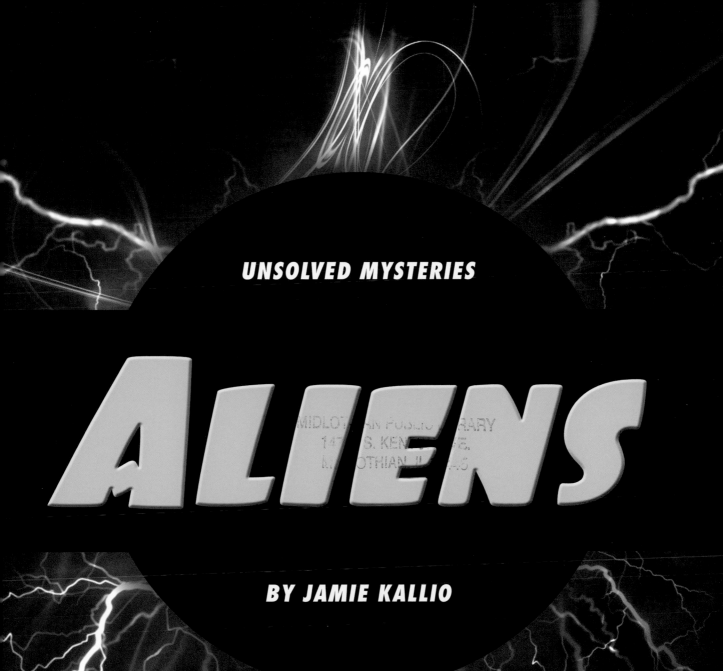

UNSOLVED MYSTERIES

ALIENS

BY JAMIE KALLIO

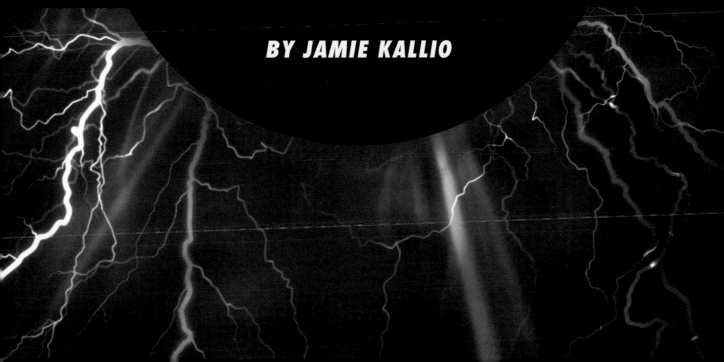

ABOUT THE AUTHOR

Jamie Kallio is a youth services librarian in the south suburbs of Chicago. She is the author of several nonfiction books for children. Kallio has never seen an alien. She is a fan of Doctor Who and would love to time travel.

The Child's World

Published by The Child's World®
1980 Lookout Drive • Mankato, MN 56003-1705
800-599-READ • www.childsworld.com

ACKNOWLEDGMENTS
The Child's World®: Mary Berendes, Publishing Director
Red Line Editorial: Editorial direction
The Design Lab: Design
Amnet: Production

DESIGN ELEMENT: Shutterstock Images

PHOTOGRAPHS ©: Albert Ziganshin/Shutterstock Images, Cover, 15;
Shutterstock Images, 5, 9, 10, 11, 17, 19, 23; Lev Savitskiy/
Shutterstock Images, 7; iStock/Thinkstock, 13; NASA/JPL-Caltech, 21

ISBN 9781634070683
LCCN 2014959756

Printed in the United States of America
Mankato, MN
March, 2016
PA02312

TABLE OF CONTENTS

ALIENS AMONG US?

On October 25, 1974, Carl Higdon was hunting in Wyoming. Higdon worked as an oil driller nearby. He often hunted in the woods. That day, his trip began as usual. Then something odd happened. Later, he described his experience.

Higdon shot his rifle at an elk. Then he started to feel strange. The bullet traveled slowly. Suddenly, it stopped moving. It fell to the ground. Surprised, Higdon picked up the bullet. He looked around him. He saw a human-like figure in the woods.

Carl Higdon believed he met an alien in the woods.

The figure came toward him. Higdon noticed that it had no ears. Its arms ended in sharp points. He spoke to the figure, which called itself Ausso. Soon, Higdon found himself in a cube-shaped **vessel**. The vessel took off into space. He saw Earth through the window. Ausso took Higdon to a small room and examined him. Then Ausso said he had failed a test. He returned Higdon to Earth. Higdon was gone for two hours. He believed that Ausso was an alien.

An alien is an intelligent being from another planet. Many people claim they have seen aliens. Some say aliens have **abducted** them. Their stories are similar to Higdon's story. Others do not think alien abductions are possible. Whether or not aliens have visited Earth, there could be life on other planets. Scientists are searching for the truth.

Is Anybody Out There?

Earth is in the Milky Way **galaxy**. The Milky Way has more than 100 billion stars. Many stars are part of solar systems. A solar system is a group of planets or other bodies that orbit a star.

Are there aliens in our galaxy? Many people think so. They believe Earth is not the only planet with life. For years,

A galaxy may contain billions of planets and stars.

people wondered if aliens were on nearby planets. Popular movies showed aliens on Venus and Mars. These planets are like Earth in many ways. Their surfaces are made of similar materials.

So far, no one has found alien life in our solar system. But the rest of the galaxy is very large. Scientists are only beginning to study some parts of it.

Researchers look for clues on planets. These clues suggest that life could exist on the planets. One clue is water. If water exists on a planet, it may support life. Researchers also look for signs of alien cultures. These are things aliens made. Radio signals in space are examples of this kind of clue. They could show that aliens exist or once existed.

Aliens in History

Other clues about alien life may come from Earth's past. Many ancient cultures told myths. These stories were passed on through generations. Many stories told of powerful beings. The beings came from the sky to visit people. Some researchers believe the stories are true. The powerful beings may have come from space. Perhaps aliens visited Earth long ago. They may have helped humans.

The Sumerians were an ancient people. They lived approximately 5,000 years ago. They wrote the first words ever written. These words mean "star god." Some experts believe the star god was an alien.

There are examples from other cultures, too. Indian myths describe flying "serpent people." Early Chinese

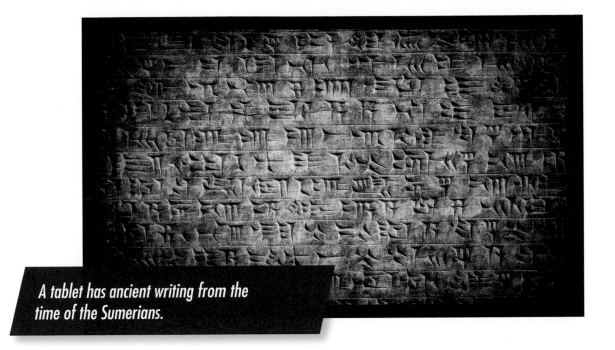

A tablet has ancient writing from the time of the Sumerians.

cultures spoke of a sky dragon. One important example comes from the Aztecs. They lived in Central America from about 1200 to 1520. One Aztec god was Quetzalcoatl. This god was half bird and half snake. He came from the sky in a silver egg. Could the silver egg have been a spacecraft?

Alien Monuments

Certain experts think aliens gave knowledge to people. They believe the aliens brought new tools. They helped people build early monuments. If this is true, aliens shaped our world.

Stonehenge is an ancient monument made of slabs and boulders.

Stonehenge is a monument in the United Kingdom. It was made thousands of years ago. Historians think it was a burial site. Stonehenge contains boulders arranged in a circle. The boulders weigh up to 4 tons (3.6 metric tons). How did people move these heavy rocks? They did not have modern machines. According to some people, aliens helped them. These researchers also think aliens helped construct the pyramids in Egypt.

No one can prove that aliens visited ancient people. But some reports about aliens are much more recent.

MYTH OR FACT?
Aliens carved the ancient Ica stones found in Peru.

This is a myth. In 1966, Dr. Javier Cabrera lived in Ica, Peru. A friend gave him a stone with a fish carved on it. The stone was made of a very hard rock. Dr. Cabrera later found 15,000 carved stones. He believed they were very old. How did ancient people carve such hard stones? They did not have many tools. Did aliens help them carve the pictures? Scientists studied the stones. They found that modern villagers had carved them.

Some people wondered if ancient aliens carved the Ica stones in Peru.

ALIEN ENCOUNTERS

William "Mac" Brazel was a rancher near Roswell, New Mexico. In the summer of 1947, he found a pile on his ranch. It contained strange **debris**. The debris was made up of rubber, sticks, and tinfoil.

An Army Air Field team took the materials. The team worked to identify the debris. One officer said the debris was from a crashed flying saucer. Newspapers reported on this exciting claim. People wondered what happened to the alien visitors. The next day,

Many people believe that aliens are coming to Earth in unidentified flying objects, or UFOs.

the story changed. Another officer said the debris was simply from a weather balloon. Weather balloons record temperatures and other information.

Many people doubted this later report. They believed that a UFO had crashed. Some also thought aliens died in the crash. In 1980, Charles Berlitz wrote a book about the debris at Roswell. He claimed the government was hiding the truth. When the government hides information, it is called a **conspiracy**.

History experts explain the Roswell crash differently. They think the debris came from a secret military aircraft. The aircraft looked different from most airplanes or weather balloons. That's why people believed it was a saucer when they saw it in the sky. Scientists have a similar view. The debris contained common materials. These materials are often used in aircraft. Alien vessels would probably use rarer materials.

Believers and Skeptics

Scientists say there is no proof of aliens visiting Earth. But some UFO researchers disagree. They believe that millions of Americans have seen aliens.

Some people believe they have proof of alien visitors. People have seen glowing rings in the soil. They say that UFOs created these rings. Many people can also describe aliens in detail. Their descriptions are often similar. Through these descriptions, experts identify three kinds of aliens. The Grays are short. They have long arms and only four fingers. Grays have very large heads and eyes. The Reptilians are very tall with greenish-brown skin.

Aliens with large heads and eyes are called Grays.

They have cone-shaped heads. Reptilians have slits for noses and snake-like eyes. The Nordics have blond hair. Their eyes are blue or light-colored. From far away, Nordics look human.

People who say they have seen aliens usually have similar stories. Many have blocks of missing time. They forget what they did for hours. Some say they have been in spaceships. Beams of light brought them aboard. Afterward, they have nightmares of aliens and UFOs.

MYTH OR FACT?
Some crop circles are unexplained.

It is a fact that some crop circles are a mystery. Crop circles are large designs in fields. Most are made in wheat or corn crops. About 250 circles appear yearly around the world. Some people believe they are alien messages. Others say they are landing areas for UFOs. Many people admit to making crop circles as a prank. But some crop circles are unexplained.

Skeptics say that abductees did not really meet aliens. They believe these people only had dreams about the encounters. People sometimes see aliens after driving for a long time. Tiredness may make them imagine being abducted. Skeptics also argue that UFOs are not spaceships. They are most likely meteor showers or airplanes flying low in the sky. One thing is true, though. Few alien sightings are pranks. Most claims are made by people who strongly believe they saw aliens.

A small number of people do make up stories about aliens. They might claim to be abducted for fame or as a joke. This kind of trick is called a hoax. One famous hoax was about a medical examination on an alien. In 1996, Ray Santilli gave a film to television stations. He said that a cameraman made it in 1947. The film showed a doctor operating on an alien. Some people thought it was from

Roswell. They believed the film was proof of a conspiracy. It showed that the government hid proof of aliens. But in 2006, Santilli confessed that it was made up. He created the film using actors and special effects.

Santilli's film did prove one thing. People are very interested in aliens. More than 11 million people watched the film. They wanted to know if aliens are really out there.

CHAPTER THREE

THE SEARCH FOR ALIEN LIFE

Have aliens visited Earth? We may never know for sure. However, scientists may soon discover life somewhere in space.

Earth-like Planets

There are billions of galaxies outside the Milky Way. Alien life may exist in some of these galaxies. Recently, scientists discovered a planet called Kepler 186f. It is trillions of miles away. This planet is called Earth's twin. Kepler 186f is about the same size as Earth. Scientists believe

Scientists use technology to search for alien radio signals in space.

there could be water on the planet. They think Kepler 186f can support life.

Kepler 186f is not the only Earth-like planet. Scientists are searching for more. One group is named Search for Extraterrestrial Intelligence (SETI). This group searches for signs of aliens. SETI uses technology to capture radio signals. Members try to identify signals from alien worlds. People help SETI from home, too. They run computer programs to find these signals.

NASA continues to probe into space. Scientists send **rovers** to Mars. NASA teams use **telescopes** to make discoveries. One is called the Kepler telescope. This telescope is very powerful. Scientists use it to look for Earth-sized planets around other stars. Astronomers believe there could be many of them. They have already found more than 1,500 **exoplanets**. Most exoplanets probably do not contain life. Yet scientists think that some of them do. Soon, people may discover alien life deep in space.

What would aliens look like? Scientists have some ideas. Some aliens might look like bugs. On Earth, bugs have strong bodies. Such strong creatures can survive in different kinds of places. They could probably live on other planets. Other aliens might look like deep-sea creatures. They could live on planets with water. A few scientists think aliens might look like humans. They could survive on a planet like Earth.

NASA sent this rover to gather information from Mars.

Many types of creatures live on Earth. Animals, birds, and people make this planet their home. Perhaps other planets have many types of creatures, too. People have different opinions about aliens. Soon, we may know the truth.

Glossary

abducted (ab-DUKT-ed) When people are abducted, they are kidnapped or taken away. Carl Higdon said that an alien abducted him.

conspiracy (kuhn-SPEER-uh-see) A conspiracy is a secret plan made by two or more people. One author says there was a conspiracy to keep aliens a secret.

debris (duh-BREE) Debris is scattered pieces of something that has broken. People found debris they thought was from a UFO crash on a ranch.

exoplanets (EK-soh-plan-its) Exoplanets are planets that orbit a star other than Earth's sun. Scientists have discovered many exoplanets that might support life.

galaxy (GAL-uck-see) A galaxy is a large group of stars and planets. Earth is in the Milky Way galaxy.

probe (PROHB) A probe is a tool for recording information from outer space. NASA uses probes to photograph planets.

rovers (ROW-verz) Rovers are machines that move around and are used to gather information. NASA sent rovers to Mars to gather samples of soil and to take pictures.

skeptics (SKEP-tiks) Skeptics are people who doubt that something is really true. Most skeptics do not believe that aliens exist.

telescopes (TEL-uh-skopes) Telescopes are instruments that make faraway objects look bigger. Astronomers use telescopes to see distant planets.

vessel (VESS-uhl) A vessel is a large boat, ship, or spacecraft. Some people believe an alien vessel crashed in Roswell, New Mexico, in 1947.

To Learn More

BOOKS

Parks, Peggy J. *Mysterious Encounters: Aliens.* Detroit: KidHaven Press, 2007.

Pipe, Jim. *The Twilight Realm: Aliens.* New York: Gareth Stevens Publishing, 2013.

Walker, Kathryn. *Unsolved! Mysteries of Alien Visitors and Abductions.*
New York: Crabtree Publishing Company, 2009.

WEB SITES

Visit our Web site for links about aliens: **childsworld.com/links**

*Note to Parents, Teachers, and Librarians: We routinely verify our Web links to make sure
they are safe and active sites. So encourage your readers to check them out!*

Index